IMPLEMENTING
COMMUNITY
POLICING
IN NIGERIA
12 CONCISE, PRACTICAL AND EFFECTIVE
COMMUNITY POLICING STRATEGIES

DR CHARLES OMOLE

DIRECTOR GENERAL
INSTITUTE FOR POLICE & SECURITY POLICY
RESEARCH (IPSPR)

MORE ABOUT THE AUTHOR
DR. CHARLES OMOLE LLB, LLM, PhD

Dr. Charles Omole is a Legal, Economic & Political Strategist, Leadership & Business Coach, Entrepreneur and Good Governance and Reform Guru. He is a Security consultant, Trainer and Strategist to businesses and governments across the world. Also, a Constitutional law scholar, he brings together an excellent academic & research pedigree and practical industry experience in a compelling proposition. He is a global expert in International Law and Organizational Transformation fields.

A first-class strategist and trainer; Dr. Omole is a world-renown expert in matters relating to Political & Economic Strategy, Corporate and National Security operations, Institutional Good Governance, Entrepreneurship & Leadership Development. He has worked in over 40 countries and advised many nations on developmental matters.

Rarely have the academia, industry, political and government proficiencies been effectively combined in one individual. He is also the **Director General** of the **Institute for Police and Security Policy Research (IPSPR)**, an independent research institute to promote collaborative research programmes and opportunities between the police, military, security practitioners, the academia and industry experts across the African continent. He has contributed to security sector reforms in dozens of countries.

With his wide-ranging experience in economics, business & finance, technology, organizational change, politics, the judiciary, national security, policing and leadership coaching, Dr. Omole combines an incredibly vast and versatile range of expertise in operational management, leadership, corporate transformation and strategic change management that makes him a formidable consultant and sought-after adviser around the world. He has been a faculty member that trained many officers of the Nigerian Police from the rank and file to senior officers (including all the CPs, AIGs, DIGs).

He is a bestselling author of over forty books on policing, politics, law, national security, leadership and faith matters.

IMPLEMENTING COMMUNITY POLICING IN NIGERIA

12 Concise, Practical and Effective Community Policing Strategies

CHARLES OMOLE LLB, LLM, PhD
DIRECTOR GENERAL
INSTITUTE FOR POLICE & SECURITY POLICY
RESEARCH (IPSPR)

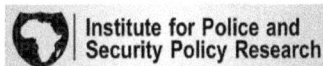

Copyright 2020

By

Dr Charles Omole

ISBN: 978-1-907095-38-2

Published by:

Institute for Police and
Security Policy Research

London . New York . Lagos

TABLE
OF
CONTENTS

INTRODUCTION

Community Policing is a policing system that proactively involves and engages the local communities in policing activities, from crime prevention, crime management to intelligence gathering.

It is a policing paradigm that can be implemented differently in different communities, cities and nations as long as the community centric approach is adopted in its overarching design.

This adaptability and flexibility of Community Policing has made its implementation difficult to comparatively capture since different nations will be doing different things all in the name of Community Policing. This factor has also made it easier for lip service to be paid to implementation when in fact nothing happens in reality.

Since 1999 return to democratic rule; Nigerian Police has been discussing the implementation of Community Policing. Strategy after strategy documents have been produced; yet this form of policing is yet to be operationalised effectively in Nigeria.

In fact, the community perception of the police has deteriorated further in the years since 1999 and confidence in the Nigeria Police Force is at an all-time low.

This book is deliberately written in such a way that all rank and file officers can read and understand it. So, I have avoided theoretical analysis and purely academic discussions. I have also avoided discussing if Community Policing is a good idea for Nigeria as there is already a consensus on that point. The book is a practical charge which focuses concisely on how Community Policing can be delivered while not giving much attention to the theoretical concepts of Community Policing, its origin and systemic merits. There are plenty of books that have already done justice to those points.

The overwhelming focus of this book is on how the Nigerian Police can operationalise Community Policing in as quick a way as possible and with the least resources expended.

The failure of the centralised national Nigerian Police to effectively operationalised Community Policing has been one of the reasons there has been increasing calls for the establishment of State or Community Police forces across the country.

This book will not address that issue specifically; but I can state categorically that the strategies in this book will work regardless of the policing management structure adopted in Nigeria in the months and years ahead.

Our research has shown that most Nigerian do not really care who control the police as long as they feel safe and their livelihoods protected from criminality.

Pervasive insecurity is what drives many to look for alternative solutions in State or Local police structures in the hope that those will provide better outcomes. The strategies discussed in this book will work regardless of whether Nigeria adopts State/Local policing structure or not.

It is safe to assume that if the current Nigerian Police get Community Policing right; the call for other forms of policing may indeed recede substantially. So, getting Community Policing right is therefore in the best interest on both the current Nigeria Police Force and the communities across the country that they serve.

It is my hope that the police authorities in Nigeria will learn from this concise book steps they can take to quickly implement Community Policing across the country.

To maintain the concise nature of this book, I have left out several elements deliberately. Those gaps can be filled later with additional engagements with the police when they are truly ready to deliver Community Policing.

After reading this book, the leadership of the police at all levels should be able to see the low hanging fruits of Community Policing implementation they can adopt swiftly to improve community relations and public perception of the police.

For those that want to study Community Policing in-depth; I have provided some Bibliography at the end of the book to signpost you to materials that can assist in that endeavour.

I have also included an Appendix that reproduces some of the core texts on Community Policing for those who may find it difficult to source the books in the Bibliography. I hope this will help give a complete picture of this subject to all readers.

Community Policing work from bottom up, but the policy framework and its establishment has to first be enforced from top down. So, leadership is needed from the Force Headquarters for this to be a reality.

The strategies in this book are as a result of years of assessment and review of policing across Africa and other developing nations. So, these are solutions that can work in any country although I have customised the analysis to fit the Nigerian peculiarities.

In the final Chapter; I listed some next steps actions leadership of the Nigerian police can take to give effect to these ideas. This include applicable backend systems that will need to be in place to support some of these Community Policing ideas.

To the leadership of the Nigeria Police Force; I hope this book will spark additional creativity to see what is possible in improving the delivery of Community Policing in Nigeria for the benefit of all. We can get this right. Yes, we can.

God bless Nigeria.

Dr Charles Omole
July 2020

One

CHAPTER 1

HISTORY OF COMMUNITY POLICE REFORM DISARRAY IN NIGERIA

Much have been written about community policing globally and in Nigeria over the past few decades. This concise book is not intended to delve into the conceptology of Community Policing.

Neither will the book spend time explaining the theoretical framework surrounding Community Policing. The

Bibliography will signpost additional materials that have already done justice to those areas.

The goal of this book is to provide a practical template on how Community Policing can be operationalised in Nigeria. A form of Ideas factory document one can say. My approach will be direct and straight to the point.

This book is written under the assumption that a decision has been made to roll out Community Policing in Nigeria by the relevant authorities. So, I will not be selling the concept but simply showing examples of how it can be operationalised easily. With all these caveats in place; how can Nigeria implement Community Policing in ways that is effective and practical.

Since 1999; there has been three Presidential Panel on police reform in

Nigeria. One under the administration of President Obasanjo. Another in 2004 under President Yaradua and then in 2008 under President Jonathan.

One thing common to all these panels is a recommendation that Community Policing should be rolled out in Nigeria. The reports of these panels (despite government White Papers being produced for two of the panel reports); were not acted on my successive governments.

This habit of abandoning reports of expert panels has made many within the Nigerian Police to be tired of talks of change and reform in an environment where nothing seems to change after each panel reports.

This 'change' or 'reform fatigue' has led to loss of inertia and a form of hopelessness that the police will ever be reformed. This has further entrenched antiquated and bad practices within the organisational system.

There are many problems and challenges facing the Nigerian Police. While I will not focus on these; I will still like to mention a few of them so as to create the correct context for readers to understand the peculiar challenges to reforming the police in Nigeria.

These challenges will help explain why there has been repeated talk of Community Policing but no practical action taken to make it effective in reality.

Many years ago, the Nigeria Police Force established in Nigeria Policing Programme (NPP). NPP was supposed to champion the operational design and implementation strategy for Community Policing. While NPP made some progress; there is still no effective outcome on the ground.

Research conducted in the University of Liverpool School of Law and Social Justice[1] has shown that a £30 million UK Department for International Development programme to improve the Nigerian police's relations with the community failed because of corruption and inefficiency among the law enforcers.

The Security, Justice and Growth Programme, funded by DFID and managed by the British Council, was set up to overcome the reluctance of Nigerians to report crimes or help the police with their enquiries.

The research, conducted by Dr Aminu Musa Audu from the University's Department of Sociology, Social Policy

---

[1] < www.liverpool.ac.uk> accessed on 30 May 2020

and Criminology, shows that despite a decade of implementation, the desired crime prevention and community safety have not been achieved – the overwhelming view of the community is that police officers in Nigeria are corrupt and that corruption has impacted negatively on their professionalism. This verdict is supported by our previous research on policing in Nigeria.[2]

According to Dr Audu; "the programme, which ran from 2002 to 2010 to train officers in Community Policing roles in 18 of Nigeria's 36 states, had failed because "members of the public do not trust the police in Nigeria on account of a huge perception of corruption." This also support our previous research findings in this area.[3]

---

[2] Dr Charles Omole has conducted extensive research on policing in Nigeria and published several books on his findings.
[3] ibid

The Community Policing policy initiative, brought in as an alternative to "top-down, coercive, non-accountable, paramilitary policing," had not been taken seriously by the police."[4]

His finding is an indictment on the management and leadership of the Nigerian Police in no uncertain term. Are the police self-sabotaging their own reform agenda? Why has delivery of Community Policing been just words and few practical actions have actually been taken. Why is such a simple and direct policy framework made to look complicated and unworkable in Nigeria?

Dr Audu further added: "The government of Nigeria, after the introduction of the Community Policing policy in 2002, sent some police officers

---

[4] Curled from Dr Audu's speech to the British Sociological Association's annual conference in Manchester.

to the UK and the US for training in the fundamentals of Community Policing.

They were then meant to ensure the transfer of the knowledge to other police personnel in Nigeria. However, only a few officers attended the overseas training and there was a lack of consistency in the training policy on the part of the Nigeria police management. In the view of police participants interviewed, such training abroad was undertaken only to achieve promotion and an overseas trip-related allowance, rather than training in its original sense."[5]

In his research; he narrated the story of a police officer who told him that many in the Nigerian Police (leadership and rank and file included) were afraid that bringing in Community Policing would

---

[5] www.liverpool.ac.uk accessed on 30 May 2020

end the benefits they got from corruption.

According to this respondent; "Some experts from UK and US came to train some of our people in the act of community policing, and they got the certificate of attendance. At the end of the day, it was an addition to their curriculum vitae. Now what happens? Nobody is ready to promote the ideals of Community Policing because it will assist not only in curbing crime among the citizens but will also do some justice to the issue of corruption in the system. The system is seeing community policing as a burden."[6]

This is now the big problem. Can the Nigerian Police leadership be trusted to deliver Community Policing? Currently, most of the officers in the Nigerian Police serve outside their ethnic origins.

---

[6] ibid

Can officers who are not familiar with the language and culture of where they are serving be able to deliver Community Policing? The culture of ethnicisation of police structures in Nigeria is not helpful to delivery of Community Policing. Certain ethic groups are accused of favouring their own people with plum postings and high-profile roles.

There is mutual distrust amongst certain ethnic champions within the police organisation (backed my ethnic politicians) which creates hidden agendas when it comes to implementation of a nationwide scheme such as Community Policing.

There are urgent and frank policy discussions that need to take place within the leadership of the Nigerian police. Who is afraid of Community

Policing in the Nigerian Police? Why have the realisation of Community Policing been a failed project in Nigeria; despite massive resources and years of trying to make it a reality?

These are issues that this book will not want to delve into (as it will distract from the focus of the book); but the concerns were raised so that readers do not think the author is oblivious to the practical challenges of police politics and management shenanigans in Nigeria.

This book starts from the premise that a decision has been made to genuinely implement Community Policing in Nigeria.

This book is a concise contribution to this endeavour by signposting some quick practical; strategies that can be implemented to deliver Community Policing.

The call for State Police in Nigeria is a reflection of the frustration of many Nigerians with the Nigeria Police Force and its inability to effectively secure the nation. Our research has shown that most Nigerians do not care whether its state or Federal Policing system as long as they feel safe and are secure in their communities.

So, it is the failure of the police to provide that security that is making most look for alternative structure (such as state police) that they feel can provide solution to their security problems. In my opinion; the greatest enemy of the police in Nigeria can be the police themselves.

Many officers do not market any good image of the police to the citizens. And the near paralysis of its management to deliver Community Policing despite almost two decades of promising reveals a form of hypocrisy and self-sabotaging antics by simply playing a lip service to this promises to deliver Community Policing.

The leadership of the Nigerian Police must now make up its mind if indeed, they want Community Policing or not.

The wave of political movement towards State and regional security outfits all around the country shows that the vacuum will be filled by others if the police leadership fails to act. The good thing is that the strategies explained in this book will work for a State/Local policing structure as well as current Federal formation.

But by taking a lead, The Nigeria Police Force can help shape the Community Policing initiative in Nigeria rather than simply responding or reacting to events and actions of other players like State governments or the politicians.

My love and affection for the Nigerian Police has never been hidden. I believe there are many excellent officers within the service. Ever since I decided to focus my research endeavours on policing in Nigeria many years ago, I have been dedicated on trying to assist the police to be better and do better to serve Nigerians. Even for me; it has been a journey full of frustration and irritation on many occasions.

On many occasions; high politics seems to be elevated above professional judgements. And I have seen fears of officers afraid to speak out or do the right things out of fear of reprisals. A professional police service is possible only when professionalism is at the core of decision making from rank and file to its leadership.

Despite the foregoing analysis of the failures within the police itself; there are many hindrances that are out of the control of the police due to its legal framework, funding challenges and operational environment. I will be looking into these in the next Chapter.

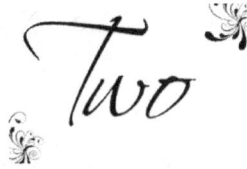

Two

CHAPTER 2

SPRECTRUM OF CHALLENGES FACING THE NIGERIAN POLICE

Although I have stated in the previous Chapter how the police can be their own worst enemy in Nigeria; there are however other challenges facing the police that are definitely beyond their control. One can go as far as saying the police were never set up to succeed. They were set up to fail.

It is clear to that Nigerians do not fully appreciate the depth and scale of the challenges facing the Nigeria Police Force (NPF).

It is easier to be critical of them, but they have not been set up to succeed but rather to fail. The constraints faced by the police are so enormous that effective policing is almost impossible unless there are changes. These constraints have metastasised into many misconduct and unprofessional behaviour by many police officers.

Despite attempts by the police institution to discipline and even sack officers that are reported, there is a never-ending pipeline of badly trained and badly cultured officers who perpetuate similar misbehaviour that replaces the sacked ones.

From recruitment, to training, to internal management, there are many challenges facing the Nigerian police.

And until these challenges are addressed, any attempt to reform he police will be like sticking plaster over a crack instead of fixing it. So, what are these Challenges?

HISTORICAL CHALLENGES
The way the Police has been emasculated historically by the military has stunted their capacity to be citizen-focused or respond to effectively manage crime and criminality.

The historical baggage the police carry, has stripped them of the principle of "Policing by Consent" which is essential for public buy-in into police operations. Historical underfunding and neglect has caused a lot of damage.

INSTITUTIONAL CHALLENGES

Corporate culture and internal discipline. No independent complaints system. The PSC has no independent capacity to investigate or police the police. Complaints against NPF officers to PSC end up being investigated by the NPF itself (though a party to the complaint), who then reports to PSC.

This is unsatisfactory. No ratings or independent Inspectorate regime that will rate police Commands or measure their effectiveness.

STRUCTURAL CHALLENGES

The way the police are organised does not promote community policing effectiveness. CPs take instructions from IGP instead of Governors. The over-centralised structure of the police does not help it to connect with communities as it should.

LEGAL/ESTABLISHMENT CHALLENGES

The legal framework of NPF need to be changed to provide security of tenure for IGP. S215(3) of the Constitution states that: *"The President or such other Minister of the Government of the Federation as he may authorise in that behalf may give to the Inspector-General of Police such lawful directions with respect to the maintenance and securing of public safety and public order as he may consider necessary, and the Inspector-General of Police (IGP) shall comply with those direction or cause them to be compiled with."*[7]

But what can the IGP do if the President gives him an order that is unlawful. Absolutely nothing. In fact, the constitution in S215(5) states: *"The question whether any, and if so what,*

---

[7] The 1999 Constitution of the Federal republic of Nigeria (As amended).

directions have been given under this section shall not be inquired into in any court."[8]

So; the IGP cannot seek judicial review of an unlawful order by the President. This by implication means the IGP has to obey ALL orders given by the President; whether lawful or not. Or get sacked.

These Legal constraints make manipulation of the police by any President very easy. The President can easily remove any IGP that does not play ball. That is why we have had about 13 IGPs in 15years.

OPERATIONAL CHALLENGES
Lack of adequate equipment and tools. Up to 40% of officers on personal guard duties. NPF does not have sufficient frontline officers because lots of them

---

[8] ibid

are on private security duties with VIPs and anyone that can afford to pay for their services.

This creates operational difficulties for the core policing functions as there is scarcity of officers.

FINANCIAL CHALLENGES

Not enough is being spent on policing by the Federal Government. We now have Policing by donating and corporate goodwill in Nigeria. Basic infrastructure and equipment does not exist in many police locations.

For instance; as of early 2020; fingerprint searches in the Police is done via manual paper searches in filling cabinets. There is no computerised system at the central registry in Lagos. It is all manual searches done on paper with hand-held magnifying glass.

Most officers buy their own uniforms and allowances are paid very late if at all. These avoidable difficulties promote subsistence corruption throughout the police estate.

ENVIRONMENTAL CHALLENGES
Wider Criminal Justice slowness & poor public recognition. The wider criminal justice system is so badly managed that police officers have also become part of the problem.

Proliferation of security outfits in Nigeria have also diluted the role of the police so much that people often get confused as to who to report certain crimes to. These disparate security agencies compete instead of cooperating.

For example, all private security firms in Nigeria are licenced by the Civil Defence Corps and not the NPF and Billions are collected annually from these firms as registration fee by Civil Defence.

Civil defence focuses on protecting its bread and butter first rather than share these information with the police in an automatic fashion.

The State Security Service and known for not trusting the police with intelligence. They simply operate in their silo most of the time. So how can the police be effective when facing these environmental challenges.

CAPACITY CHALLENGES
Ongoing Training and validation not widespread. Inadequate recruitment and initial training. The recruitment process into the police is so ineffective that it will be a miracle if we get any good officers in the future.

Garbage in, is garbage out. You can finish a prison term for armed robbery in Aba today and join the police in Lagos tomorrow. As long as you do not declare your conviction; there is no way the police will know.

NPF recruits contain all manner of criminals and criminally insane individuals that the training regime that could have weeded them out has also been compromised.

Heads of police training colleges have tales of "Instruction from above" commanding that ALL recruits-in-training must be passed, even though more than half failed the course or examination.

This ensure poor quality on-boarding of officers which inevitably leads to poor officers on the job.

LEADERSHIP CHALLENGES

Too many IGPs in succession. Hence lack of continuity and strategic focus. Too many tactical responses and little strategic focus. The lack of security of tenure due to the legal challenges of the way the police is setup noted earlier leads to a revolving door of IGPs in succession.

So IGPs are not in post long enough to make strategic plan and impact. In fact, those that spend more than a year as IGP lived in fear that they could be sacked at any moment that they fail to make any long-term strategic plans.

Giving certainty of tenure to IGPs will make them more effective and more independent of politicians.

POLITICAL CHALLENGES

Too much political interference in policing in Nigeria. This demotivates good officers as political patronage becomes a basis for promotion and benefits.

This political interference has also decimated the ranks of Specialist Officers in the NPF; who are often requested to become personal security details by Governors and public office holders (against NPF rules). Once the police losses such officers to politicians; they usually never come back to their hands-on specialist posts afterwards.

As can be seen from these Ten Challenges; simply recruiting more officers will not solve the problems. In fact, the current approach is merely re-enforcing mediocrity.

Changing and transforming policing in Nigeria, require that attention is paid to all these challenges for the benefit of the nation.

Three

CHAPTER 3

Practical Community Policing Strategy for Nigeria - 1

POLICE LIAISON OFFICERS STRATEGY

Police Liaison system is an effective form of Community Policing which has never been practiced in Nigeria before. This will require existing officers at Divisional Police level to be appointed as liaison officers to various community institutions such as schools and hospitals. The liaison officer will need to visit the institutions monthly for a few hours to do some floor walking and engagement.

In schools, the Liaison officers could be part of the school assembly that day or visit classrooms

to pass on safety messages. They will dispense crime prevention and basic security tips to pupils. Local salient crimes and trends and prevention techniques will be shared.

How to identify specific crimes like grooming, child abuse and even rape will be explained to the children. The name and phone number of that officer will be made available to the children and institutions. Over time, a relationship of trust will develop between the liaison officers and their institutions. This helps to build community bond

The liaison officers will become the first point of contact by these institutions whenever security related problems arise. They will become well known by these local institutions and pupils (in the case of schools) tend to find it easier to supply information to a face they have come to know over months than to a new officer they have never met before.

The first step in implementing this strategy is to compile the names of all applicable institutions and their numbers per police division.

Then Secondly; the officer to institution ratio will need to be decided. Depending on the type of community, it may be one officer per institution of one officer overseeing several institutions.

Thirdly, full training will need to be provided to all police officers on what this role will entail and how to make a success of it.

Next, the officers will be introduced to their various institutions and a schedule of visits is designed and agreed.

This police liaison role should be undertaken by no more than half of police officers in each divisional area. This is to ensure operational flexibility for the divisional leadership. These allocated officers should be given reprieve from reposting for an agreed period to allow them time to fully get into the swing of things and develop these relationships fully.

This strategy will incur minimal cost as the officers are already in place in every community. It is just a matter of allocating them to the identified institutions; train them up and they deploy them.

This liaison role should take on average 1-4 days a month of an officer's time depending on how many institutions are allocated. For most officers, this will be one day a month. Multiple allocated institutions can be visited in one day.

Better community understanding and visibility will result from these liaison roles. Better intelligence picture can also be developed. More importantly, citizens will begin to see the police as friendly and as community champions. This helps to build trust and confidence with the public over time.

Four

CHAPTER 4

Practical Community Policing Strategy for Nigeria - 2

LOCAL POLICE CONTACT NUMBER STRATEGY

It is customary for nations and even States within a nation to have an emergency numbers citizens call when needed. But for community policing an additional approach is expedient.

Each Local Government Area (LGA) can have dedicated number to access the local police. This will be number(s) that can help achieve the following:

- A number to call when there is local emergency.

- A number that can be used to reach the police in non-emergency situations.

- A number that can be used to pass on vital information to the police.

- A number the community can use to make suggestions to the police.

On the backend; the call answering can rotate seamlessly between police stations within each LGA on a rota basis. Designated and trained officers will take turns in being on duty to answer the calls.

The local element of this number will not only speed up police response but will help develop better rapport between the police and the local communities.

The local nature of this number will also help the police to identify local trends in crime and incident mapping that will guide enforcement actions.

This number should be divert-able to mobile phones so officers can even take calls while on the move. Ideally this should be a 24hrs 7days a week facility. But it is possible to start by making it working hours only with a message facility for after hours.

Five

CHAPTER 5

Practical Community Policing Strategy for Nigeria - 3

POLICE ON THE BEAT STRATEGY

Street patrol has been a traditional form of Community Policing for over a century. In fact, street patrol existed before Community Policing was coined as a term in policing.

Also known as "Bobby on the Beat or Foot Patrol"; street patrol is the most reassuring policing strategy for any community. It creates visibility and also deters opportunistic crimes.

I accept this form of policing can be human resource intensive. That is why it can be targeted to start with. Frequency of patrol can be expanded over time.

Police can conduct street patrol only at very busy periods for the communities. Market days, rush hour, weekends and so on can be specifically targeted. Foot patrol also helps to keep officer fit.

With many officers' overweight and unfit; street patrol helps to improve stamina and overall physical fitness of officers. It also helps the police to gather real intelligence about what is going on in the community.

For officers that are new to the community; foot patrol helps them to get familiar speedily with the area. There are so many benefits to the "Police on the Beat" strategy that its implementation should be a no brainer.

If done properly; this strategy can have a deterrence effect on crimes in the community with the criminals not sure if they will encounter police foot patrol while committing crime.

Specific areas of the community can be targeted as well. So, it does not mean every street in a community must be patrolled on foot. Central and busy areas should be prioritised. This strategy can be complemented with vehicular patrol by the police as well.

Six

CHAPTER 6

Practical Community Policing Strategies for Nigeria - 4

COMMUNITY EVENTS ENGAGEMENT STRATEGY

This strategy involves the police organising community events as well as going to be part of other local events organised by other institutions.

Here are a few of the ways this strategy can be implemented:

1. Police can organise "OPEN DAYS" every quarter when people from

the communities are welcomed as visitors to police stations. They will be shown round and basic snacks can be provided. This will make the station more welcoming for them to visit to report a crime if needed after.

2. Police can organise Community Shows where school children will be able to come and try on police

uniforms and see inside police vehicles while crime prevention lessons are given out to parents and adults. A local musician or comedian can be on hand to support the police.

3. Police can approach organisers of local events in the community for a kiosk or spot to be given to the

police to display information about what the police does in the community.

This community campaign strategy can take multiple forms but the overarching goal is to bring the police closer to the community through constant and consistent community contact.

Local police can also engage their communities through activities that will improve the communities such as gutter clearing and sanitation campaign. Police can also help fix abandoned community projects or facilities.

This engagement strategy will endear the police to the people and help improve the profile and perception of the Nigerian Police.

Police-community panels or committees can be set up at the Divisional level as necessary to promote these community engagements.

Seven

CHAPTER 7

Practical Community Policing Strategy for Nigeria - 5

CIVIC EDUCATION STRATEGY

This strategy requires police to work with the local education authorities to include practical crime prevention training in the curriculum of schools starting from the primary school level.

This can be delivered by regular class teacher and not police officers. The aim is to sensitise pupils on issues of crime prevention and how to identify crime, especially emotion and psychological crimes.

Officers may also make reference to the content of this aspect of the curriculum (by explaining things further) when they visit schools as part of their liaison role.

 As part of this strategy, the police can publish their own education materials and distribute in schools and the community at large.

This strategy can complement a future police recruitment strategy. With an effective civic education campaign; interest in police can be created in your folks and thus a pipeline of future recruits can be created.

Eight

CHAPTER 8

Practical Community Policing Strategy for Nigeria - 6

CRIME PREVENTION CAMPAIGN STRATEGY

One of the main accusation of Nigerians against the police is the fact that the police always show up after crimes have been committed and the criminals long gone.

The police are seen as reactive and never proactive when it comes to crime detection. So, this strategy requires the police to conduct street by street crime prevention campaigns. This will include door to door leaflet campaign disseminating crime prevention information in the community.

This will also require the police to visit every victim of domestic crimes in the community to pass on information on how to avoid being re-victimised and signpost residents to support groups and facilities available in the community and the state at large.

Police need to be seen as proactive in helping to prevent crimes rather than just trying to solve crimes. As Robert Peel once said; *"The hallmark of a good police service is not in its crime solving capabilities but in that crimes never occur in the first place"* (my paraphrase). So, a good crime prevention campaign strategy should help reduce and prevent crime from taking place rather than simply trying to solve an increasing volume of crimes being reported.

This crime prevention campaign will also include the use of Police Public Notices (PPN). This involves police putting up crime avoidance notices in crime hotspots in the community. These notices will be on street posts and prominent places. Examples are:

Police can also give away free security marking pens and other products to the community to mark their assets so that it will be easier to trace owners if stolen.

Nine

CHAPTER 9

Practical Community Policing Strategy for Nigeria - 7

SPECIAL CONSTABULARY AND LOCAL UNDERCOVER AGENTS STRATEGY

One of the powers that the Inspector General of Police have under the law which has never been used in recent memory is the power to create "Special Constables".

These will not be paid officers but volunteers who will be given some police training. These will be people who have their day job but willing to volunteer an agreed number of days a year with the Nigeria Police Force. They will be uniformed and can be deployed to do low level police works in the community.

Special Constable recruitment is open!

Recruitment closes Sunday 3 May
Find out how
#YouCanMakeADifferenceToo:
www.nottinghamshire.police.uk/Specials

The closest example I can give is with the Federal Road Safety Commission's (FRSC) 'Special Marshal' scheme. This allows ordinary citizens (after some training) to conduct basic road safety tasks.

This frees us the full-time marshals to do more serious safety tasks. These special marshals are unpaid but they have helped to improve the community link between the FRSC and the communities. The police can do the same.

These Special Constables are volunteers that police will manage directly. The rank and file of the police can be enlarged locally at little or no cost to the Nigerian Police. Special Constabulary helps to demystify the police and make them more connected to the community.

The special constabulary is a form of serving the community like no other. The special constabulary is a force of trained volunteers who work with and support their local police in our various communities.

Special Constables will come from all walks of life - they are teachers, market petty traders, taxi drivers, secretaries, or any number of other careers - and they all volunteer an agreed number of hours of their time each week and month to the local police.

Many Nigerians actually want to give something back to their community. But the added benefits include; learning new skills and gaining valuable experience for a CV; for a personal challenge; or to learn about the police before committing to a full-time career with the Nigerian Police.

Becoming a special can also help volunteers develop self-respect and self-confidence; improve their communication skills; and learn more about their community.

Aside from or in addition to the special constables; the police can also recruit local volunteers as informants. They will be managed directly at the Area Divisional Level for better control and accountability.

These will be folks going about their normal daily job but who would have been trained on what to look out for and feed back to the police. All this will of course be done with utmost discretion. I accept that trust in the police may need to rise to a much higher level before many Nigerians volunteer for this role to help the police.

But it can be rolled out on a case by case basis in different communities rather than a national implementation.

Ten

CHAPTER 10

Practical Community Policing Strategy for Nigeria - 8

INTELLIGENCE-LED POLICING LOCAL ACTIVATION STRATEGY

This strategy requires Intelligence Hubs to be established at every Police Area Command in the country. This will need to be technology driven.

Police will create an Application for Mobile Phones that will allow residents to send pictures, videos and other information to the police. This will have to be set up as part of an Intelligence-Led Policing initiative in the community.

I have already written extensively on how Intelligence-Led Policing can be deployed in Nigeria. So, I do not wish to repeat all the details again in this book.

My book on this subject can be obtained from all good bookstores globally.

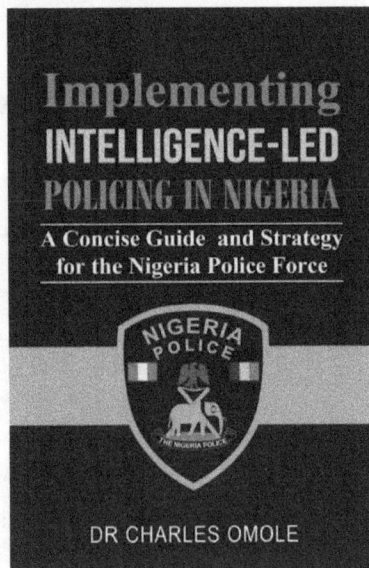

What is Intelligence-Led Policing in brief

Intelligence-led policing (ILP) is a business process for systematically collecting, analysing, and utilising intelligence to guide law enforcement operational and tactical decisions.

ILP aids law enforcement in identifying, examining, and formulating preventative, protective, and responsive operations to specific targets, threats, and problems.

It is important to note that ILP is not a new policing model; rather, it is an integrated enhancement (and deliberate Joined-up of isolated existing tools) that can contribute to public safety.

The concept of intelligence-led policing describes an emerging approach to policing that 'began to currency' (Smith

1997) in the early 1990s at the twilight of the 20th century.

The terrorist attack in New York on 9:11 is a vivid reminder of what happens when intelligence is kept in silos by different security agencies. Information on all the hijackers where on different databases of the various security agencies but none was talking to each other to help form a complete picture of the threats that existed.

So, a complete picture was impossible. Many countries have since learned from that major error by trying to integrate and mine all their data and intelligence in joined up ways. But this is not the case in Nigeria.

The ILP process can provide a meaningful contribution by supporting the Police's existing policing strategy, whether it is community-oriented policing, problem-oriented policing, or other methodology.

The ability to collect, examine, vet, and compare vast quantities of information enables law enforcement agencies to understand crime patterns and identify individuals, enterprises, and locations that represent the highest threat to the community and concentration of criminal and/or terrorist-related activity.

The most extensive and insightful definition of the ILP was given by Smith as follows:

"Intelligence-led policing is a term that has only begun to gain currency in the last three to five years. For this reason, it lacks a single overarching definition.

Most would agree, however, that at its most fundamental, intelligence-led policing involves the collection and analysis of information to produce an intelligence end product designed to inform police decision-making at both tactical and strategic levels.

It is a model of policing in which intelligence serves as a guide to operations, rather than the reverse. It is innovative and, by some standards, even radical, but it is predicated on the notion that a principal task of the police is to prevent and detect crime rather than react to it".

Through this method, the Police can prioritise the deployment of resources in a manner that efficiently achieves the greatest crime-reduction and prevention outcomes. (Like all other security agencies, the Police must prioritise to be more effective).

Intelligence has always been part of police work. However, in the traditional policing approach, intelligence is used to aid investigation after a crime incident.

This approach has been referred to as policing-led intelligence (Cope 2004). In contrast, intelligence-led policing (ILP) repositions intelligence from back-stage to front-stage of policing.

This is necessary as emphasis is now in guaranteeing and preserving public safety has moved away from mere enforcement to risk and crime prevention. So, intelligence is supposed to direct the actions of the police in a more accurate fashion.

ILP encourages the use of both overt and covert information gathering from the community. This approach also maximizes the use of available resources and partnerships, such as those capabilities available through informants, the civic society and local/State intelligence centres.

The reasons for the rapid development and enthusiastic adoption of some form of ILP model in developed economies and polities have been identified by one of the world leading scholars in this area as follow:

a) the desire to explore new approaches to crime control;
b) ineffectiveness of the standard model of policing.
c) paucity of evidence that a reactive and investigative approach to policing has any impact on the level of crime;
d) financial constraints imposed on police departments during the rapid increases in recorded crime in the 1970s and 1980s;

e) availability of new technologies that increased the volume of information and capacity of information retrieval and analysis services available to police chiefs, helped spur interest in analytical approaches to problem identification and definition commonly known problem oriented policing;

f) lack of convincing evidence that community policing is effective in reducing crime;

g) problem-oriented policing lacks the evidentiary base for widespread adoption.

ILP is executive implementation of the intelligence cycle to support proactive decision making for resource allocation and crime prevention.

In order to successfully implement this business process, Zonal leadership must have clearly defined priorities as part of their policing strategy.

At its core, ILP helps leaders make informed decisions to address policing priorities. These priorities can include issues such as crime prevention, crime reduction, case management, resource allocation, case clearance, anticipation of future threats, or crime problems. This process provides guidance and support to the Police leadership, regardless of the type of priority established.

ILP Operational Concept

For ILP to work, there has to be Steering from the Leadership on the following:
- A clearly defined Priorities
- The Policing Strategy

Individual junior officers CANNOT be expected to lead on ILP, although they are needed to implement it. This is a crucial point to note.

There is no single method for implementing ILP. The size of the State Command, complexity of the threat environment, the local political environment, and resource availability within each command varies greatly across the Zonal commands on the Nigerian police.

Therefore, how ILP implementation "looks" within each State or Zone may vary accordingly. (E.g, a very rural command can rely more on human Intelligence, while another in urban area may rely more of technology sourced intelligence).

However, adopting ILP as a philosophy and business framework, to whatever degree is appropriate, can and will improve the effectiveness and efficiency of any policing organization.

The end goal of ILP is to enhance proactive policing efforts and further the positive outcomes of law enforcement actions toward reducing crime and protecting the community against a variety of threats.

Eleven

CHAPTER 11

Practical Community Policing Strategy for Nigeria - 9

"POLICE-AWARE" SIGNAGE CAMPAIGN STRATEGY

A new system of 'POLICE AWARE' stickers should be rolled out in the country. Each patrol vehicle will be given supply of these stickers.

Officers must be encouraged to display these stickers anywhere they have attended to damaged public or private properties that are in public spaces.

This will include broken down cars that does not have owner present, damaged shops or break-ins. This will have the effect of making hitherto hidden police hard work more visible to the public.

This will promote greater awareness of hidden police work thus improving positive perception and support for the police

A protocol will need to be written on its use and the steps officers should follow

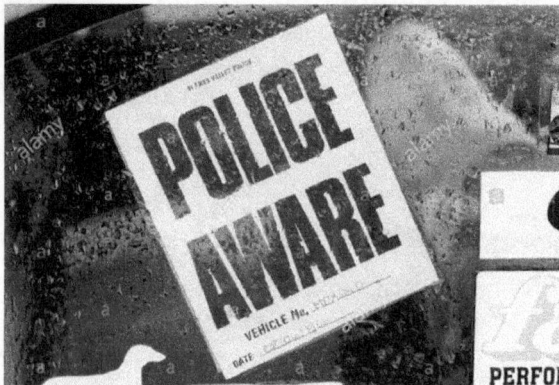

to use it. The officer will have to write codes for his station and himself on the stickers.

This will make it possible to trace the officer who issued the sticker in case there is an enquiry.

This creates greater visibility for the policy in the community. And the hard work of officers is more appreciated.

In addition to the Police Aware stickers; the police can also use Incidents Board to solicit public information where there have been crimes committed in certain areas of the community. Road accidents, stabbings, robberies and other public order offenses can be investigated with this addition tool. This reassures the community that the police are actively working incidents.

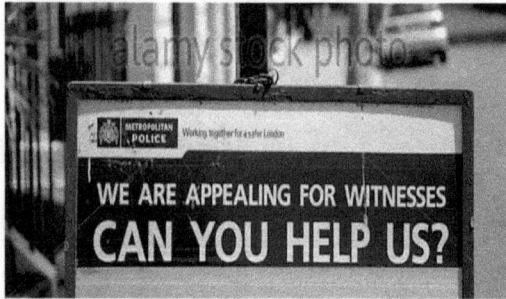

The Nigerian Police should employ the use of public notices to request public help in accident or crime spots as well as give public warnings of coming major incidents such as road closure.

This has a psychological impact of making police actions more visible and improve public appreciation of police work.

Twelve

CHAPTER 12

Practical Community Policing Strategy for Nigeria - 10

POLICE-LOCAL SECURITY/VIGILANTE LIAISON STRATEGY

This mechanics for this strategy to be implemented is already taking shape in several states across Nigeria.

With states now setting up various security outfits such as "Amotekun" by the Western Nigerian states; the foundation for this strategy is already being laid all over the nation. The police need to utilise these state outfits to obtain intelligence and deal with low level crimes.

A protocol need to be agreed with each state on how the police will work with each of these outfits to safeguard communities.

If communities know these outfits work collaboratively with the police; security reassurance may be provided for residents who may otherwise live in fear.

Synchronising the strategies in this book is very important if effective policing is to be achieved.

For example, the police could limit the use of the suggested Special Constabulary in cities and urban areas; while engage the local security outfits and vigilantes for rural areas and bushes.

This will create a simpler architecture and avoid duplication or over-policing of the same community.

The rules of engagement have to be agreed with these outfits. The police also have to be careful of the political shenanigans of state Governors who may want to use these local outfits for political purposes.

Thirteen

CHAPTER 13

Practical Community Policing Strategy for Nigeria - 11

POLICE LIVING IN THE COMMUNITY ENGAGEMENT STRATEGY

This is a long-term strategy that requires a deliberate policy by the police leadership to encourage and support more of their officers to live within the communities they serve. The idea of "Barracks" is rooted in the needs of the colonial masters to have easy access to security personnel in an emergency. Hence if they are all housed in one location; security personnel can be called out more quickly in an emergency. Below is a picture of the Victoria Island Police Barrack in Lagos. As you can see; it is a disgrace and slum. Most police barracks are like this now.

Colonial governments need for coercive force is what birthed the idea of barracks where police and other security personnel are housed away from the communities and segregated in giants housing estates that have now become slums all over Nigeria.

The barrack idea is now obsoleted for civil policing globally. Officers need to be encouraged and supported to live amongst the people.

This keeps communities safer knowing armed police officers live in their streets. Gathering of intelligence will also be easier with officers living in the community.

A typical police barrack is an eyesore and a disgrace to the esteemed profession of policing. The police leadership need to demolish these barracks and provide incentives for officers to live in their various communities.

This will create greater bond between the police and the people. It will deter some criminal activities as well.

This is s strategy that may take a longer time to deliver but the policy framework need to start now.

Fourteen

CHAPTER 14

Practical Community Policing Strategy for Nigeria - 12

POLICE LOCAL RECRUITMENT CAMPAIGN STRATEGY

Police recruitment exercises can be conducted at the local level by a central team. The idea of folks travelling miles to a specific local to join the police can disconnect them from the community link vital for community policing. As a suggestion; the Nigerian police can introduce a new category of officers from the next recruitment campaign.

Currently Nigerian police officers are classified as either General Duties (GD) or Special Duties (SD) officers. A new category can be introduced and that can be called Community Duty (CD) officers. Such officers will never be transferred out of their communities unless in exceptional circumstances.

Adverts for police recruitment should be done more locally than through national publications.

This will create new group of officers who will make knowing their local communities a career-long endeavour. CD officers can be moved around only within an Area command. This will make them available for local liaison roles for example.

Fifteen

CHAPTER 15

PRACTICAL NEXT STEPS

Community policing is a policing philosophy that emphasizes community-oriented problem solving to reduce and prevent crime. It should be a police management tool and an organizational strategy that promotes a cooperative partnership between police officers and members of the communities they serve.

The goal is to collaboratively resolve problems and improve community safety and security through police partnerships with residents, businesses and other stakeholders.

What happens next to deliver the dream of effective Community Policing in Nigeria.

I belief the following steps (and some more) will need to be considered urgently by the leadership of the police. These steps are in no particular order.

1. The Inspector General of Police (IGP) need to set up an Implementation Panel (IP) for Community Policing in Nigeria. This panel MUST be chaired by an outsider and someone not a police officer. This is crucial if the IGP want to be told the truth about challenges and obstructions to his instructions.

2. The Chair of the panel MUST report directly to the IGP and nobody else. This will minimise any attempt to sabotage the project by vested interests within the police organisation.

3. Examine and assess internal procedures that can hinder implementation of Community Policing. An example is the transfer system that moves officers too frequently. A community liaison officer for example will need stability to build relationships which will not happen if he is transferred too frequently as currently the case.

4. Piloting of some of these strategies may be prudent. So, target states must be identified for the piloting of these strategies. The pilot should not exceed one year before

review and evaluation of effectiveness. Lessons learnt can then be used to improve the wider roll out nationwide.

5. While many of the strategies have no additional cost; some do. So, the remit of the IGP's panel will include costing the exercise. And the police leadership need to find the necessary funding accordingly.

6. A monitoring team need to be set up by the IGP that will ensure quality assurance nationwide and monitor compliance with procedures as well as receive feedbacks and suggestions from both the public and frontline officers.

7. A Community Policing related internal award system can be instituted to motivate and reward commands that are doing well as exemplars and to encourage others.

8. A Change/Role Impact Analysis exercise will need to be conducted on frontline officers to assess the impact of new Community Policing strategies on roles, deployment strategies and daily routine of officers.

9. Some of the strategies can be implemented directly by the Nigeria Police Force; others will need working with local stakeholders including local security apparatus and vigilante groups. This will give added value to the state security apparatus

being set up by some states across the country.

10. There will be a need for technological upgrade within the police organisation to exploits some of these strategies. Databases will need to be built and Applications may need to be procured. The IGP implementation panel can be tasked with coming up with ideas of funding sources for these deliverables.

11. Local and Community structures will need to be setup to effectively manage some of these strategies. So each Police Division or Area Command can have a Community Safety Board (CSB) that will include all relevant stakeholders in that community. The CSBs will

then have a State-wide body made up of the Chair of all the CSBs in the State. This will enable comprehensive communication and ownership of outcomes as well as challenges.

12. The IGP and his leadership team need to come up with a Theme or Mission Statement for the Community Policing scheme. This should capture in simple terms the goals of the scheme and its intended outcome. An example of a mission statement could be something like:

"Becoming a Community-focused police service, proactively working for a safe and secure communities and become the pride of all Nigerians."

13. The IGP Panel should help draft the Assessment Criteria for the Community Policing initiative on an ongoing basis. This can be both Qualitative (such as number of specified crimes reported) and Quantitative (such as detection Ratio) criteria. These criteria will be used to assess, measure and improve the operations of the Community Policing schemes.

14. Community Policing should become a central part of police training in all police colleges for new officers. But a programme of continuous training on Community Policing need to be put in place for existing officers.

15. Community Partnerships should be encouraged and promoted to all Divisional Police Officers. Part

of their job assessment should be how effectively that have been able to partner with the communities. To enhance residents' formal collaboration in achieving public safety, the Police should maintain working relationships with all key community based organizations and other local government agencies.

The actual implementation of these strategies may vary slightly to reflect community culture. So, there may be differences from one region to another region of the country. But the overall driving principles will be the same.

To keep this book concise, I have avoided putting too many details about these strategies in this book. But there is enough to showcase the strategies. Details of how each strategy will be implemented should be part of the IGP's panel remit. This will allow esoteric considerations to be taken into account for each geo-political region.

Community Policing can work in Nigeria regardless of whether there is State Police or not. The current Nigeria Police Force can make these strategies work if there is true willingness to get it done.

Especially given the little to low cost implication of many of the strategies. A lot has been said about Community Policing in Nigeria for a long time.

It is time to start doing some things to gain momentum in the right direction and improve community relations all over the country.

Nigerian Police can indeed become the envy of Africa; but the journey starts now.

Finally, it needs to be understood that Community Policing is not about who controls the police. It is about the links and connection that the police have with the communities in which they operate.

You can have State police but no Community Policing. And you can have Federal Police with better Community Policing strategies in place.

So, while the debate may rage on about establishment of State police; Community Policing can be in place in fully implemented regardless.

BIBLIOGRAPHY

- Braiden, Chris. 1992. "Enriching Traditional Police Roles." Police Management: Issues and Perspectives. Washington, D.C.: Police Executive Research Forum, p. 108.

- Community Policing Consortium. 1994. Understanding Community Policing: A Framework for Action. Washington, D.C.: Bureau of Justice Assistance. Reprinted in Willard M. Oliver, ed. 2000. Community Policing: Classical Readings. Upper Saddle River, N.J.: Prentice Hall.

- Correia, Mark. 2000. Citizen Involvement: How Community Factors Affect Progressive Policing. Washington, D.C.: Police Executive Research Forum.

• Flynn, Daniel. 1998. Defining the "Community" in Community Policing. Washington, D.C.: Community Policing Consortium

• Goldstein, Herman. 1993. The New Policing: Confronting Complexity. National Institute of Justice, Research in Brief. Washington, D.C.: U.S. Department of Justice. Reprinted in Oliver, Willard M., ed. 2000. Community Policing: Classical Readings, 71–80. Upper Saddle River, N.J.: Prentice Hall.

• Hough, Laeatta M. 2002. Hiring in the Spirit of Service: Definitions, Possibilities, Evidence and Recommendations. St. Paul: Community Policing Consortium

• Adeyemi, A. A. (1993) "Information Management for National Development, Planning and Security" in T. N. Tamuno

- L. Bashir, E. E. O. Alemika and A. O. Akano eds. Policing Nigeria : Past, Present and Future (Lagos : Malthouse Press Limited).

- Akano, A. O. (1993) "The police, Rule of Law and Human Rights : The police Perspective" in T. N. Tamuno et al eds. Policing Nigeria.

- Alemika, E. (1986) "Criminal Justice Principles and Nigerian police Prosecutorial Disposition" Nigerian Journal of Policy and Strategy 1(2): 1-17.

- Alemika E. E. (1988) "Policing and Perceptions of police in Nigeria" police Studies 11(4): 161-176.

- Alemika, E. E. O. and Chukwuma I.C. (2000) - police-Community Violence in Nigeria (Centre for Law Enforcement Education, Lagos and the National

Human Rights Commission, Abuja, Nigeria)

- Ali, G. (2008), police and Human Rights Abuse in Nigeria. A seminar paper presented in Department of Sociology, Ahmadu Bello University, Zaria.

- Claire de Than, etal (2003), International Criminal Law and Human Rights. New York: Thomson, Sweet and Maxwell.

- Guelke Adrian, 2001. "Crime, Justice and the Legacy of the Past," in Crime and Policing in Transitional Societies. (Seminar Report). Johannesburg, RSA: Konrad Adenauer.

- Comassie, A.I. (1990), Discipline Superior police Officer. A paper presented at the seminar for Area Commanders and Assistant Commissioners of police held at the police Staff College, Jos. March 19 -23.

- Comassie,A.I. (1996), The making of the Peoples' police. Lecture delivered at the National Orientation Agency, Abuja.

- Nwankwo,C.D. etal. (1993), Human Rights Practices in the Nigerian police. Constitutional Rights Project, Lagos.

- Odinkalu, C. (2002) Ed. Hope Betrayed: A report on Impunity and State-Sponsored Violence in Nigeria. Geneva: World Organisation Against Torture and Centre for Law Enforcement Education.

- Tamuno, T. N (1970) The Police in Modern Nigeria: 1861-1965. Ibadan: Ibadan University Press

- Innes, M., and Thiel, D. (2008) Policing terror In Newburn, T. (ed.) Handbook of policing. Cullompton: Willan. pp 553-579.

APPENDIX 1

To assist those not able to obtain the Bibliographies for further reading I will recite below some key principles about the Theory surrounding Community Policing so as to deepen the knowledge of those not familiar with the concept. The footnotes cite the sources of these recitations.

UNDERSTANDING THE COMMUNITY POLICING PHILOSOPHY[9]

Community policing is used worldwide, but understanding of the Community Policing term varies in different countries. If you would ask 100 people what the community policing is, then you would get 100 different answers. There is also a continued discussion about the understanding of this

---

[9] Curled from the publication of Conclusions of the European Commission Project Promotion of Crime Prevention through Community Policing in Talsu Police Department, Latvia.

philosophy and its application in various cultures of the world, which is not always as simple and understandable as it was in old democracies.

However, irrespective to various opinions and theories, public support of police work has been sought for long and it has been admitted that community policing is a process which continues its development in line with time and topical requirements of the public.

Tom Potter, former Chief of Portland Police, is believed to be the founder of community policing philosophy. He developed basic principles of this philosophy at the time when he was walking the beat as a young policeman.

Others believe that the source of this tradition lies in nine principles of modern police work which were defined by Robert Peel approximately one hundred and fifty years ago.

Repeated discussion on importance of community policing became topical after the terror acts in the United States of America and Europe, when it became apparent that acquiring and summarising information on an early stage may be a very useful tool allowing the police and other law enforcement services to duly eliminate the threat of radicalism and terrorism.

Also, the assassinations of publically known people (for example, assassination of the director Theo Van Gogh in the Netherlands) and riots and acts of vandalism (for example, the events in Great Britain in summer 2011) make the police services look for even new ways to control the situation in the field of public security. The situations in various countries and regions are, of course, different and also the models of police work in the modern society are called and interpreted differently: police work in democratic society, police work according to human rights principles, community policing, problem-oriented police work, vicinity police work, police work based on the needs of population, value-based police work and other ways how modern and effective police work methods are understood throughout the world.

The public has changed and continues to change, and the police should follow such changes. The issue of various groups of public is especially topical at the moment – for the purpose of police being able to control the security situation in the vicinity, an appropriate approach to each group is required.

Community policing methods are becoming increasingly popular throughout the world because representatives of police become more aware of the contradiction between what they are doing and what they should do according to the public opinion.

Though the police are performing well and in a professional manner, and are succeeding in catching criminals and detecting offences, the public is not satisfied with police work and has difficulties in understanding its importance.

Therefore, the aspects which are important in everyday life of people and which increase the sense of security at the place of residence should be emphasised more in the police work.

DEFINING CHARACTERISTICS
OF COMMUNITY POLICING[10]

The Community Policing Consortium defines community policing as *"a collaborative effort between the police and the community that identifies problems of crime and disorder and involves all elements of the community in the search for solutions to these problems."*

Community policing is based on the premise that police alone cannot control crime and disorder and promote residents' quality of life (Community Policing Consortium 1994). In community policing—in contrast to traditional policing—the public's involvement is viewed as a "co-producer" of community safety and wellness (Whitaker 1980; Parks et al.

---

[10] From article by Lorie Fridell, Director of Research, Police Executive Research Forum

1981; Parks et al. 1982). Community policing also expands the role of police beyond crime fighting to maintaining order and promoting improved living conditions for residents.

While traditional policing has been characterized by reactive responses to crime, community policing emphasizes proactive problem solving to prevent and otherwise control crime (Sparrow, Moore, and Kennedy 1990; Sparrow 1988).

The goals of community policing are to reduce crime and disorder, promote citizens' quality of life in communities, reduce fear of crime, and improve police–citizen relations (Community Policing Consortium 1994).

These goals are achieved through three essential efforts: community engagement, problem solving, and organizational transformation. The following discussion focuses on how each of these elements is understood in the community policing context and raises key questions about their effective implementation.

Community Engagement

Sir Robert Peel said, "the police are the public and the public are the police" (Braiden 1992). This statement reflects a key tenet of community policing: the police should not be separate from, but rather joined in partnership with, the community.

A major impetus for the move away from traditional policing was the recognition that the police cannot control crime and disorder alone. With community policing, the police and community are expected to co-produce safe and healthy communities (Parks et al. 1981, 1982).

The partnerships can and should serve to empower residents to take responsibility for their neighbourhoods. As stated by Kelling (1988, 2–3), "police are to stimulate and buttress a community's ability to produce attractive neighbourhoods and protect them against predators."

Important to this relationship are agency activities that promote interaction and familiarity with jurisdiction residents.

Agencies generally achieve stronger links with citizens using myriad approaches including long-term assignments of officers to specific geographic areas; foot and bike patrols; mini-stations in communities; community meetings; citizen police academies; and other forms of outreach such as Police Athletic

Leagues, educational programs in schools, and citizen volunteer programs. But, however important these outreach programs are for promoting a strong police-community relationship, other activities are required to cement a true partnership with the community. One key activity is collaborative problem solving.

In a true partnership, the police and citizens make important decisions together about agency policies, practices and direction. This level of citizen involvement in the workings of the department might take several forms (for instance, residents' participation on advisory councils to the chief or their involvement in hiring, evaluating, and/or promoting personnel; developing agency policies; or reviewing complaints).

Agencies should form partnerships not only with residents but also with organized groups and private and public agencies. These organized entities are stakeholders in a healthy community, as well as potential resources for addressing community problems.

They include public and private service agencies (for example, housing agencies, other public assistance agencies and non-profit groups serving high-need groups), interest groups (for example, the Urban League, Mothers against Drunk Driving, neighbourhood organizations), and public works agencies.

Any agency that wants to gauge the effectiveness and potential of its police-community partnerships should be prepared to answer a number of key questions that have been raised about these partnerships across the United States:

- In what ways are agencies reaching out to communities to facilitate familiarity and trust?
- Are agencies moving beyond these outreach efforts to truly engage the community as partners?
- Do residents have sufficient trust in the police and understanding of community policing to become and stay involved?
- Is the role of involving the community relegated to a unit or team of officers, or is community involvement a core principle of the department, underlying all that it does?
- Are agencies successfully engaging in partnerships with organized groups and private and public agencies to cooperatively address issues of crime, disorder, and quality of life?

Problem Solving

The second element of community policing, and an objective of police partnerships with communities, is collaborative problem solving. In problem-oriented policing, police work with residents, organizations, and agencies to identify and solve community problems related to crime, disorder, and the quality of life.

But problem solving is not just a mechanism for linking with the community and developing trust; it is good policing, as Herman Goldstein, the father of problem-oriented policing, explains. "Smarter policing in this country requires a sustained effort within policing to research substantive problems, to make use of the mass of information and data on specific problems accumulated by individual police agencies, to experiment with different alternative responses, to evaluate these efforts and to share the results of these evaluations with police across the nation" (Goldstein 1993, 5). Problem solving is essential to effective prevention.

With this tool, police are not merely responding to the same locations and individuals over and over to address crime; they are addressing underlying problems that can eliminate, or at least reduce, future occurrences.

While police could conceivably conduct their problem solving in isolation, their effectiveness is greatly enhanced when the police partner with residents, organized groups, and agencies. The community's first critical task is to work with the police to identify the crime, disorder, and quality-of-life issues residents want to be addressed. Police all over the country have found that citizens' priorities may be very different from those that police might identify; both sets of priorities can be addressed and ordered in a partnership.

The community can be helpful in gathering critical information to determine the nature and scope of the problems being analysed for priority action (Eck and Spelman 1987; U.S. Department of Justice 2001, 2002). The community is then involved in working with the police to identify and implement viable responses to the problems.

APPENDIX 2

NIGERIAN POLICE RANKS

Key Nigerian Police Ranks in descending order:

- Inspector General

- Deputy Inspector-General of Police

- Assistant Inspector-General of Police

- Commissioner of Police

- Deputy Commissioner of Police

- Assistant Commissioner of Police

- Chief Superintendent of Police

- Superintendent of Police

- Deputy Superintendent of Police

- Assistant Superintendent of Police

- Inspector of Police

- Sergeant Major

- Sergeant

- Corporal

- Lance Corporal

- Constable

OTHER BOOKS BY DR OMOLE

Dr Omole has published over forty books, some of relevant ones are the following:

1) Spiritual and Practical Steps to Commanding Value

2) Breakthrough Strategies for Christians in the Marketplace

3) The Marketplace Leadership Capsules

4) How to win Political Elections

5) Financial Intelligence for Christians in the Marketplace

6) Implementing Intelligence-Led Policing in Nigeria

7) Supporting Good Governance in the Nigerian Police Force – Vol 1

8) Police Ethics and Professional Conduct

9) The Nigerian Police-Public Relationship

10) Secrets of Speaking Truth to Power

11) Implementing Community Policing

A full list of Dr Omole's books are available on Amazon and other online Bookstores.

For more information about Dr Charles Omole, Kindly email:
Info@Charlesomole.org

www.charlesomole.org

The Institute for Police and Security Policy Research can be contact at:

Info@IPSPR.org

www.ipspr.org

OFFICER NOTES

OFFICER NOTES

OFFICER NOTES

OFFICER NOTES

OFFICER NOTES

OFFICER NOTES

www.ingramcontent.com/pod-product-compliance
Lightning Source LLC
Chambersburg PA
CBHW021342290326
41933CB00037B/343